FALLING INTO Dance

DANCE AND CHOREOGRAPHY INSPIRATION

ONCE UPON A
Dance

Ballerina Konora * Teacher Terrel * Stella Maris

Once Upon a Dance

Prop-Based Movement Stories (ages 3+)

Tammy the Troll: A Dance in the Forest

Dance-It-Out! Creative Movement Stories

Eka and the Elephants (ages 4+)

Dayana, Dax, and the Dancing Dragon

Belluna's Big Adventure in the Sky

Brielle's Birthday Ball

Mira Monkey's Magic Mirror Adventure

Princess Naomi Helps a Unicorn

Fenix and the Firework Fliers (ages 5+)

The Grumpy Goat

Sadoni Squirrel: Superhero

Petunia Perks Up (also River's Dreary to Dreamy Day)

Sora Searches for a Song

Freya, Fynn, and the Fantastic Flute

Frankie's Wish

The Cat with the Crooked Tail

Danika's Dancing Day

Daryl and the Dancing Dolls (ages 6+)

Andi's Valentine Tree

Ella's Dance Debut

Ballet and Body Awareness for Young Dancers

Dancing Shapes (ages 6+)

More Dancing Shapes (ages 7+)

Nutcracker Dancing Shapes

Dancing Shapes with Attitude (ages 8+)

Ballet Inspiration and Choreography Concepts

Dance Stance (ages 8+)

Falling into Dance

Ballerina Moments: Dance Insights, Ideas, and Inspiration

Ballerina Wisdom for Dance and Life (ages 12+)

Poses for Creative Movement and Ballet Teachers

Konora's Shapes

More Konora's Shapes

Journals

Dancing Shapes

Ballerina Dreams

Dance Inspiration

Dedicated to

🩰 Stella Mongodi, for bringing *Dance Stance* and the *Ballet Inspiration and Choreography Concepts* series to life so fantastically.

🩰 Karen, Aaron, and AJ for all the support and enthusiasm for falling.

Falling into Dance: Dance and Choreography Inspiration
(Series: Ballet Inspiration and Choreography Concepts for Young Dancers)

© 2024 ONCE UPON A DANCE
Illustrated by Stella Maris Mongodi, www.stellamarisart.it
Layout and cover design by Stella Maris Mongodi

Library of Congress Control Number: 2024901582

Paperback ISBN: 978-1-955555-62-3
Hardcover ISBN: 978-1-955555-63-0
Ebook ISBN: 978-1-955555-61-6

Juvenile Nonfiction: Performing Arts: Dance
(Juvenile Nonfiction: Concepts: Body; Juvenile Nonfiction: Careers)

First Edition

Royalties donated to charities through 2030.

WHAT HAVE YOU FALLEN INTO?

Hello Fellow Dancer,

As a dancer, you belong to a unique society. No matter where you go, you can always make new friends through dance. Whenever you dance or take a class, you meet and connect with others and expand your connection to the dancing world.

Whether you dance for fun or for a career, the skills and friendships you develop through dance will serve you for a lifetime.

Dance is like a gorgeous, multilayered cake stuffed with delicious fillings such as jam and cream, then finished with icing, swirls, and superb decorations. All the ingredients work together to make a wonderful treat.

The first layer of the dance cake, posture, is covered in our book *Dance Stance*.

Kittina

Falling into Dance

Dance Stance

Bookcrasher

There's a lot more learning to stack on, but this book skips to the swirls and twirls, the embellishments and decorations—dancing with joy, expression, and enthusiasm. It's about the happy accidents we experience when we avoid a fall or fall gracefully, safely, and with style.

Although posture is the base layer, you can read the books in any order you like. I hope my advice offers inspiration and food for thought. (Maybe I mention food so much because dancers are always hungry from all that exercise, hee-hee.)

This book is not a substitute for in-person training, which is necessary if you want to pursue dance seriously. This is less of a how-to book and more of a maybe-try-this book. Not all ballet styles agree with the fundamental advice given here. Some styles might say something entirely different. Use what makes sense for you, and feel free to ignore what doesn't. And even if you're not aiming to be a professional dancer, I hope you'll appreciate my advice and anecdotes.

I've put some action items and technique instructions in "Tips from a Ballerina" so you can come back to those later.

Konora

I

SO HERE WE ARE AGAIN, FOLKS!

I am a ballerina and I love to dance. I practiced for many years to become an expert dancer. I spent four years in three different trainee programs before I was hired as an apprentice with a ballet company. It's hard to succeed as a professional dancer, and I'm lucky to have climbed as high as I have on the ballet-career ladder.

I started dancing when I was just one year old. Because my mom loves dancing, she signed me up for movement classes before I could even walk.

Coordination of anything physical, such as sports or dance, is complicated and takes time.

Even walking takes serious practice to get right.

I crawled and walked later than most babies and couldn't even stand when other toddlers my age were already taking their first steps.

When I finally got up and started moving, do you know what I could do ALL the time? I could fall—spectacularly!

THE QUICK AND DIRTY GUIDE TO DANCE STANCE

In my welcome note, I mention dance stance is our ballet cake's base layer (it's also our first book title).

Since posture is essential to everything we do, let's take a minute to think about our basic stance.

We want to straighten and lift.

Focusing on opposing forces in the body is one way we improve posture. Imagine lifting your belly button up to your neck and sending energy out through the top of your head and down to the floor. At the same time, let your shoulders fall and spread wide.

This is your starting dance stance.

BALLERINAS' FANCY-FRENCH VOCABULARY:

∝ Relevé [rehl-i-VAY]: raise (raised)

∝ Passé [pah-SAY]: passed (passé is the movement, retiré is the position; both words are used)

∝ Retiré [reh-tee-RAY]: withdrawn

∝ Grand Battement [grawn baht-MAHn]: big beat (might also hear grand battement jeté)

∝ Tendu [tawn-DOO]: stretched (might also hear battement tendu)

∝ Dégagé [day-gah-ZHAY]: to disengage (might also hear battement dégagé or battement jeté)

∝ Rond de Jambes [rahn-de-zhahm]: bend

∝ Pirouette [peer-oh-wet]: twirl (whirl/spin)

2

THE CARPET WAS CALLING, BUT I DIDN'T LISTEN
(WHY YOU SHOULD SPEND MORE TIME ON THE FLOOR)

Falling a lot can be frustrating, but here's the thing: falling is a super-duper, extremely important part of dance. All that falling we do as toddlers helps us become better dancers. If I had my training to do over again, I'd spend a lot more time falling down.

As I thought about falling, from the whys and hows to the ways we use falling concepts as tools for technique and choreography, I remembered how I fell in love with dance late compared to many dancers. Around age twelve, I'd mostly quit dancing because it took up so much time and I wanted to try other activities. I thought I'd be a scientist, so I guess you could say I accidentally fell into dance as a career.

While I'm a professional dancer in a ballet company, about half of our performances are contemporary. In ballet (or classical dance) performance, you repeat many of the same graceful jumps and spins. In contemporary dance, there's a lot of floor work—falling, rolling, flipping, crawling, turning, oozing, stacking—and finding unique shapes and movements on the ground. I'm grateful that I took contemporary and modern dance classes in addition to ballet. I don't think I'd be where I am today if I hadn't explored a variety of movement styles.

This book is inspired, in part, by what companies actually perform these days. Many ballet companies bring in a number of contemporary choreographers.

So many of the women I trained with were talented ballet dancers, but most companies are looking for dancers who excel in several styles.

TIPS FROM A BALLERINA 2
TRY THE DIS-COMFORT ZONE
(AKA NERVOUS NELLY NEIGHBORHOOD)

Dance schools often don't want their students to take outside classes in case a different studio or teacher changes your technique.

Looking back, I disagree with this philosophy. Every teacher has a unique way of teaching and sequencing combinations. Learning the same moves in different ways and hearing new language to describe them has often improved my technique.

Moving from one dance genre to another is challenging, but I think exploring a variety of styles and moving in different ways has made me a better dancer. Learning new patterns, combining steps in varied ways, and trying new moves altogether means I now learn quickly: my brain has practiced converting new movement I see into something I create.

And it's certainly given me a deeper well to draw from when choreographing!

I encourage you to step outside your own comfort zone and explore. Summer intensives are a great time to do this. You'll also gain a better sense of how you fit into the broader dance world and how likely it is that you'll be able to land a job in a fiercely competitive market.

If extra classes aren't possible, try a new teacher.

While it feels great to stay in your comfort zone, branching out can give you a new perspective. For example, when I was young, one teacher always told me to rotate whenever I lifted my leg. When I tried a new teacher, he used the word "spiral" instead. While I know those are basically the same thing, the word spiral just clicked, and I found more rotation.

3

ARE POINTE SHOES BLOCKS OF FALLING DOOM? (YES. YES, THEY ARE ☺)

Okay, we've reviewed some ballet basics. Let's digress for a minute and talk pointe shoes. Maybe you've never heard of pointe shoes, but it's a big topic of life for me, now that I dance in a company.

Pointe shoes look fancy covered in satin. They have ribbons that crisscross and tie at the ankle and are harder than regular ballet shoes. Older dancers wear pointe shoes to give the effect of floating on air as they dance on the tips of their toes.

When I was old enough, I started learning how to dance in pointe shoes. As with anything else, it took lots of practice, and I went through many, many pairs of shoes as I learned how to be graceful en pointe.

Get ready to turn the page, and prepare to gape! I'll show you the shoe collection from my first few years of pointework! (And no, they don't smell very good.)

Image by Olena Vecchia Pittura
(Photo by Once Upon a Dance)

READY, SET ... POINTE?

I know, most of us can't wait to get our first pointe shoes. I mean, are you even a real ballerina without those?!

But you should be at least eleven years old and take class three or more times a week before getting pointe shoes.

I remember being one of the last kids at my level to start working en pointe. My teacher didn't think I was ready (and she was right!). Remember the story of the hare and the turtle? Turns out, slow and steady really does win the race! So, no need to be a speedy hare and mess everything up. Just take it slow and enjoy the ride!

When you are ready, it's important to get your pointe shoes fitted by a professional so you can be sure you have the right shoes and toe padding. We don't want to end up with mushy toes, right?

Teachers should supervise and stick to a few exercises at the barre for the first few months, as students need to strengthen their muscles slowly to avoid injury.

And it's not just foot strength. You'll need strong legs and core plus good turnout to balance in pointe shoes.

Don't be fooled by a ballerina's smile! They may look like they're gliding on a cloud, but trust me, they're sweating like crazy underneath those tutus!

And do you know what dancing on those tiny points, called boxes, means?

While it means our legs and feet look long and elegant, and we can spin more efficiently—it also means that we often slip and fall!

Last summer, I did this gorgeous, amazing, oh-my-goodness-killed-it attitude turn, and as I came down ... SPLAT.

It happens to all of us.

Falls happen, even for expert ballerinas. It's unavoidable in this business, especially when you start dancing in pointe shoes.

During one *Nutcracker* show, two of my friends slipped and landed on their bottoms at precisely the same moment. I was so confused, because I saw only one dancer fall, and the sound was much louder than expected.

But they knew the drill: the show must go on! They both quickly got up and carried on with our Marzipan dance.

TIPS FROM A BALLERINA 4

BALANCE-BOOSTING TRICKS

When we relevé, the natural tendency is to let our shoulders fall back. It helps to imagine that the lift starts in your hips and pelvis. Imagine lifting yourself from the outer sides of your underwear. It also helps to keep a very slight up-and-over feeling, as if you were sniffing something yummy in a hot pan.

Use opposition energy (pulling in two different directions). Imagine a seatbelt running from your shoulder (especially the side where a leg is off the floor) to your opposite hip. Maybe the seatbelt is inside your skin. Now tighten it up just a little and see if you feel more stable.

To stay balanced, think of the weight focused between your big toe and the toe next to it, where the toes meet the foot. Feel the outer edges of your big toe and your pinky toe pushing gently into the ground. This works whether you're in relevé or flat on the ground.

Before you relevé or let go of the barre, lock your arms in position. Arms tend to get too wide or too far back when we struggle to balance. Bring your fingers a little closer together if they're in first or fifth to see if that offers more stability. If they're above your head, be sure they're not farther back than the hairline on your forehead.

If arms are to the side, be sure they are wide enough that your shoulders don't feel pinched, only long and strong.

Imagine a glass of water on the top of your head. You should notice your neck reaching taller with a little more energy and oomph to keep it from falling. This should also help your overall neck and chin alignment.

4

ALL THE FALLS

So, yes, falls happen. Dancers can fall on their knees and even fall on their faces.

Over my years on stage and in audiences, I've seen dancers

- falling down
- falling in
- falling on
- falling back
- falling off
- falling through
- falling over

I've even seen a head-over-heels fall!

Like everything else in this world, if we practice and anticipate our falls, we're less likely to get injured. If we plan for them, we'll know how to pick ourselves up and carry on with the show.

5

TRAIN TO FALL

Learning how to land after a fall can make it less scary because we're already prepared. Even thinking about falling means we'll be less shocked if it happens.

Dancers practice falling so they won't hurt themselves when they topple over accidentally.

And dancers aren't the only ones who practice falling. This type of training is great not only for dancers, but for actors as well. My brother spent an entire week of theater summer camp learning how to fall safely and be funny while doing it. These silly falls are called pratfalls.

It's also the very first thing you learn when you start skating!

Are you ready to try some falls with me?

Ok, time to practice!
Let's try some falls:

Bend your knees and arms on the way down so you never land on an extended leg or arm.

Aim to land on your side, ideally taking some of the fall on your bottom or your thigh when you first contact the ground (that's where we are most padded!).

3

Try to relax: tense body parts get hurt more easily. Think how much easier it is to break an uncooked noodle than a cooked one.

4

Don't let one body part take all your landing force. To spread out the impact, try to roll as you connect with the floor.

5

Tuck your chin and protect your head if your head is involved.

FALLING STARS
(HOW TO SHINE EVEN WHEN YOU TRIP ON STAGE)

If you're doing a solo, pretend you meant to fall, and you might fool everyone.

For group pieces, remember most of the people are there to watch someone they know. They aren't even looking at you! I can't tell you how many times I've thought I've had the biggest, most absolute disaster onstage, and somehow my mom and dad were the only ones who noticed.

Every situation is different, but here are a few options:

◦ Get up quickly and carry on (casual style).

◦ Roll offstage if you're close to the wings so you can stand up offstage and jump back into the choreography (stealth style).

◦ Dance or roll on the ground for a minute, then get up in a more dance-like way (I-meant-to-do that style).

But don't do this if you're, say, a snowflake in a fast-paced group number of sixteen! Safety first: you need to make decisions that will keep you and others onstage safe.

TIPS FROM A BALLERINA 6

STOP BEING AN INDOOR PLANT

When COVID-19 hit, I was in Pacific Northwest Ballet Professional Division. The Artistic Director, Peter Boal, told us to walk to keep in shape.

He suggested we look for stairs, hills, and rugged terrain to help us practice shifting weight, keeping our balance, and working our feet and ankle muscles. Keep this up for a lifetime, and it will make you more steady on your feet and less likely to fall when you're an adult.

Hit the Snow! Walking in snow is also a great way to build strength, flexibility, and mobility in your ankles. The next time you have a snow day, take it outside.

33

Let's practice some more.

- Start down low like a frog—bent knees out to the side with your hands touching the ground.

- Fall sideways, aiming for your shoulder.

- Try to roll over onto your back.

Hey! You just learned a modern dance move.

One other thing that will help you fall with more control and take fewer accidental falls is simply building strength in your muscles.

When you take a class, swim, walk, bike, ride a horse, or play sports, it keeps you strong.

6

FALLING CHARACTERS

Now you know how to fall, so you're less likely to get hurt.

Let's turn to choreography and have some fun. I'd like to explore using falling intentionally in dance as if we're choreographers (people who create dance sequences).

We could use many types of falls to help explain our characters: SLUMP, SHRINK, FLOP, DROP, SLIP, or T$_{R_{I_P}}$

When I danced in *Cinderella*, the stepsisters constantly flopped or tripped as part of their characters' personalities, while Cinderella was very graceful.

What kind of other characters could intentionally fall as part of the choreography?

7

FALLING WITH PURPOSE

Using your imagination is so important when you perform. Giving yourself motivation for movement makes it much more interesting to your audience (and you).

Choreographers also use falling to create feelings.

Let me show you what I mean. Let's start by thinking about objects falling. Imagine using your body to show each of these situations:

- A bridge collapsing

- Bubbles falling

- A cake sagging

- Feathers floating

Each situation feels different, even though they're all falling objects. Why don't we try it right now? Try falling like each of these. Remember to fall safely the way I showed you.

Now, let's explore a few more falling objects and how it feels to fall like them:

    ᴄᴜ Stones sinking in a lake

    ᴄᴜ Waves crashing on the shore

    ᴄᴜ Towers toppling

Can you think of more examples of falling objects? Do they fall in a particular way? How does it feel to fall like them?

You can add your personal list and observations here:

8

FINDING INSPIRATION

Everything falls. What goes up must come down, whether it's you jumping or a rocket ship flying to the moon.

Falling is inevitable, but it has many different qualities depending on whether we're jumping, soaring, or taking off like a rocket.

Imagine you are a choreographer in search of inspiration for a new dance. Choose one of the ideas about falling from the last few pages. What kind of movement or dance story would you like to tell?

We could decide to have the falling object be the very end of your dance and work backward. What made the thing fall?

A quick example (but then you have to make up your own story!): I end the dance as a feather in free-fall.

How did I get there?

Here's one possible story:

 ᢙ I'm a feather asleep on a bed.

 ᢙ A dog runs into the room, grabs a pillow, and
   spins it around.

 ᢙ I fall.

 ᢙ I float to the ground, but I'm unhappily out of control.

Can you make up your own story?

Let's brainstorm other types of falling as a choreographic exercise.

Some of these are things you can't see or touch. We call these **abstract ideas**. Here are a few you might already know:

- Falling apart
- Falling in love
- Falling to pieces

Some of them aren't very nice:

- Falling ill
- Falling unconscious
- Falling victim

Brainstorming different ideas is how some choreographers start to think about a new dance. We've used the falling concept as an example, but you could use this type of process for all kinds of dance ideas.

If you need inspiration, get out a pen and paper. Writing might not seem like part of a dancer's job, but it can help you create the idea, which is sometimes (but not always) the hardest part. Remember, you can work backward, and when you think you're done, go one level further: ask *why* one more time to see if you can get deeper into the story.

A Fell Stroke
(Bad Luck)

LET YOUR HIP FALL

While we're thinking about falling energy, here's a lesson it took me years to apply.

"Drop your hip" was a correction I heard quite a bit. When I finally learned to do it, my full-body placement improved.

Passé is a ballet movement used to start many other steps (retiré is technically the position and passé is the movement to get there and back, but you'll hear both terms to describe standing on one leg with one knee out to the side and the big toe touching near the other knee). In this movement, dancers tend to lift the active hip, but the opposite is what you want. Let your hip relax down any time your leg is in the air.

Try a grand battement: kick out a straight leg while making your working-leg hip feel heavy. This should help you send your leg out straighter and keep your torso better aligned.

With those hips more even (both vertically and horizontally), every step, balance, and turn will be a little easier. It's sort of funny that if we let one body part fall, we'll be less likely to fall down.

TIPS FROM A BALLERINA 8
EYES FORWARD

Letting your hips relax improves technique, but two things you don't want to let fall are your eyes and your chin.

Our heads are heavy, so looking down can topple us. Keep your chin lifted and your eyes looking forward or even slightly raised. This will have an added bonus of conveying confidence and compelling people to look at you!

While occasionally watching yourself in the mirror is a great tool, avoid the habit of doing this too much. You don't want to depend on the mirror for self-correction or remembering the choreography, and you won't be able to perform with full-out emotion if your eyes aren't coordinated with your movements.

LET YOUR FOOT FALL INTO PLACE

You want to return your moving foot to the standing-position home base and revisit the same strong starting position with almost every barre exercise, from tendus to degagés to rond de jambes.

Be careful, there are many ways to distort your landing into or through first or fifth position. Watch for these common mistakes:

- Leaving your heel up
- Curling your foot
- Leaning more toward the outside or inside edge, especially if you pass through first position

You want both side edges of your foot to have equal pressure when you slide out in tendu, brush through in a cloche, and even as you move across the floor and jump.

9

ONE BIG DANCING WORLD

Choreographers get their ideas from things falling in nature, too, like the zooming fast-falling star in an open sky or the cool and splashing flicks of water from a waterfall.

Sometimes choreographers make up happy dances about the weather:

- Soft snowflakes falling gently to create a blanket of quiet white

- Raindrops falling from the sky and pitter-pattering on the sidewalk

- Leaves falling from the trees and swirling in the wind

They even make dances about the seasons falling away as the months pass: winter, spring, summer, and fall. In fall, the leaves fall from the trees, swirling in the wind on the way to find stillness on the damp Earth.

As choreographers, we sometimes feel pressure to create new stories and movements, but I find it comforting to think that children all over the world have danced like a falling snowflake just like me, that we dancers are all connected, and that dance has persisted as civilizations rise and fall.

Movement connects generations and connects us to our friends around the globe. Each night, children all over the world snuggle under the covers, coldness fading as their bodies' warmth collects under the blanket.

The rise and fall of our breath helps us relax
so we can fall asleep
and fall into dreamland.

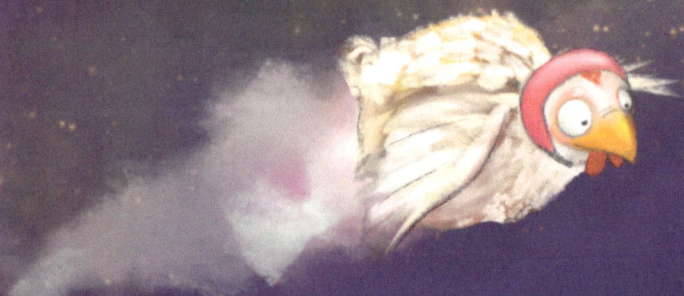

HERE'S HOPING THINGS FALL INTO PLACE

We are happy when things fall into place, especially when it's something that takes a long time to achieve, like a pirouette—the fancy ballet spin.

But practice and effort are required.

To successfully do a pirouette, you must remember many things you've already practiced:

- Balance on one foot in a high relevé
- Turn out
- Passé with a pointed foot
- Control your arms
- Keep your torso square and aligned
- Relax the standing hip
- Spot with a level head

There are so many building blocks before you can even get to a realistic attempt!

Have patience with yourself.

Success can be more satisfying when you work for it.

This idea that success is sweeter when there's more to overcome isn't limited to ballet, and many people in history have made this observation.

The author Thomas Paine observed 200 years ago,

> "the harder the conflict,
> the more glorious the triumph."

And even our successes are only temporary because we'll probably think of new goals each time we make progress. There's always something to improve upon. I've probably taken 2500 dance classes throughout my life, and I'm still learning all the time.

TIME TO SAY GOODBYE
(BUT ONLY FOR NOW!)

Thank you for exploring dance
and choreography with me!

I wish you soft landings and
joyful mistakes and missteps.

I hope that you never stop striving to improve.

For more tips from a
ballerina, check out the
other books in this series:
★ Dance Stance: Beginning
Ballet for Young Dancers

And Coming Soon:
★ Turning It Around (2025)
★ Jumping Into Dance (2026)

P.S. MY FAVORITE REMINDERS...

- Remember, everything is hard in the beginning.
- Be kind and patient with yourself as you tackle new challenges, explore new ideas, and enjoy different experiences.
- Find joy in your learning.
- And perhaps most importantly, remember to have fun along the way.

Until our next dancing adventure,
Happy Dancing!
Love,
Konora

Kittina
Poulette

Thee End

THE END

(WE END OUR STORIES THIS WAY IN HONOR OF MY GRANDPA.)

P.S.
THERE ARE 119 "FALLS" IN THIS BOOK.
TAKE A MINUTE TO APPRECIATE
ALL THE DIFFERENT MEANINGS.
THE ENGLISH LANGUAGE IS CRAZY!

WE'D LOVE TO CONNECT!

If you enjoyed our book, please ask a grown-up to take a minute to review it on Amazon or Goodreads. It really helps people take a chance on our self-published book.

My mom, a dance teacher before COVID-19, spent so much time learning about books and design the last few years, and we are donating royalties from this book to the arts (until 2030). It means the world to her to hear that people appreciate our stories.

If you know a dance teacher or studio, please let them know we have book fundraisers available. And folks can follow us on social media or subscribe to our newsletter to learn more about us:

@Once_UponADance (Instagram)
OnceUponADanceViralDancing (Facebook)

www.ONCE UPON A DANCE.com

OTHER SERIES BY ONCE UPON A DANCE

DANCING SHAPES
AGES 6+

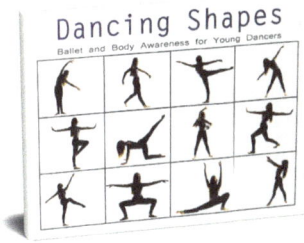

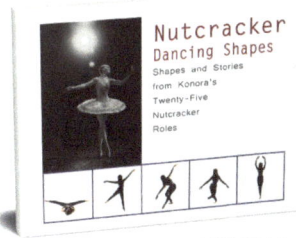

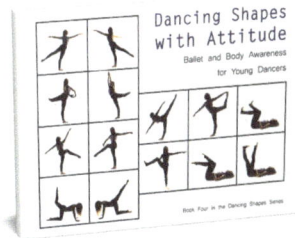

COMING SOON:
DANCING SHAPES WITH CATS

BALLERINA MOMENTS
AGES 12+

JOURNALS

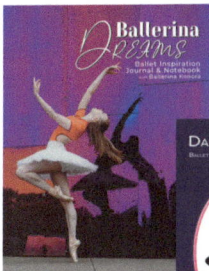

COMING SOON:
BALLERINA BLISS
BALLERINA GARDEN

DANCE-IT-OUT!
AGES 4+

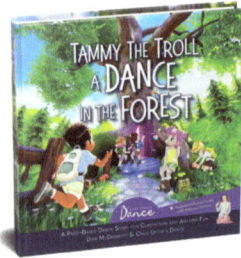

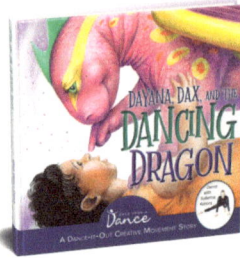

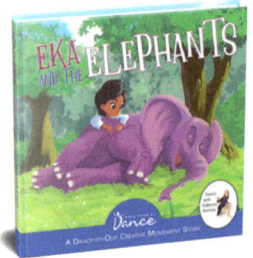

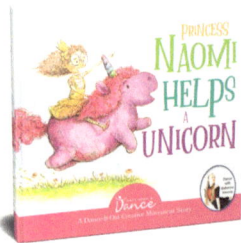

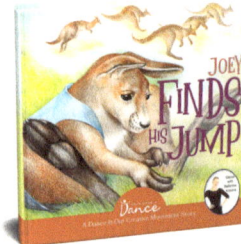

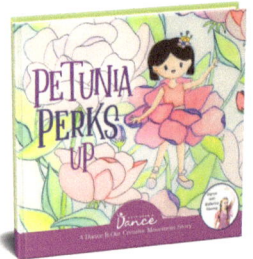

Tammy The Troll: A Dance in the Forest

Dayana, Dax, and the Dancing Dragon
A Dance-It-Out Creative Movement Story

Eka and the Elephants
A Dance-It-Out Creative Movement Story

Princess Naomi Helps a Unicorn
A Dance-It-Out Creative Movement Story

Brielle's Birthday Ball
A Dance-It-Out Creative Movement Story

Sadoni Squirrel: Superhero
A Dance-It-Out Creative Movement Story

Joey Finds His Jump
A Dance-It-Out Creative Movement Story

Belluna's Big Adventure in the Sky
A Dance-It-Out Creative Movement Story

Petunia Perks Up
A Dance-It-Out Creative Movement Story

www.OnceUponaDance.com
WATCH FOR BONUS SUBSCRIBER CONTENT

DANCE—IT—OUT!
AGES 5+

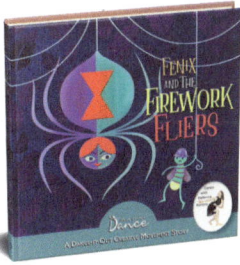

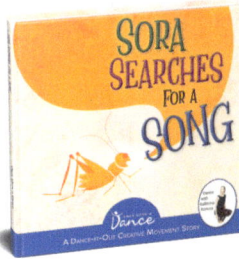

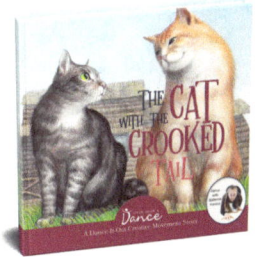

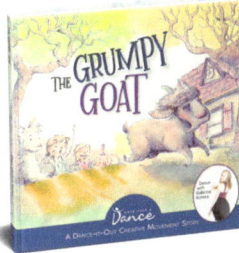

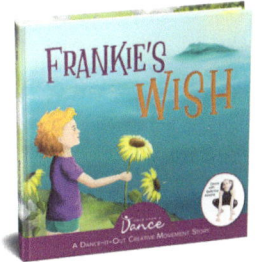

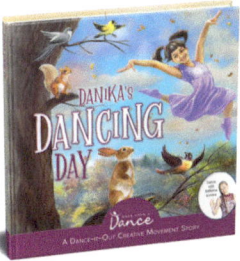

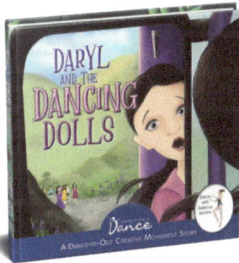

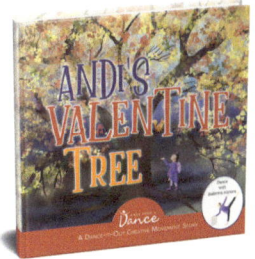

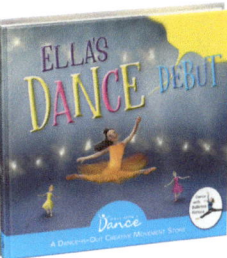

Fenix and the Firework Fliers
A Dance-It-Out Creative Movement Story

Sora Searches for a Song
A Dance-It-Out Creative Movement Story

The Cat with the Crooked Tail
A Dance-It-Out Creative Movement Story

Freya, Fynn, and the Fantastic Flute
A Dance-It-Out Creative Movement Story

The Grumpy Goat
A Dance-It-Out Creative Movement Story

Frankie's Wish
A Dance-It-Out Creative Movement Story

Danika's Dancing Day
A Dance-It-Out Creative Movement Story

Daryl and the Dancing Dolls
A Dance-It-Out Creative Movement Story

Andi's Valentine Tree
A Dance-It-Out Creative Movement Story

Ella's Dance Debut
A Dance-It-Out Creative Movement Story

ONCE UPON A
Dance

Milton Keynes UK
Ingram Content Group UK Ltd.
UKHW050730010424
440402UK00002B/3